Dedicated to our
weird and wonderful families

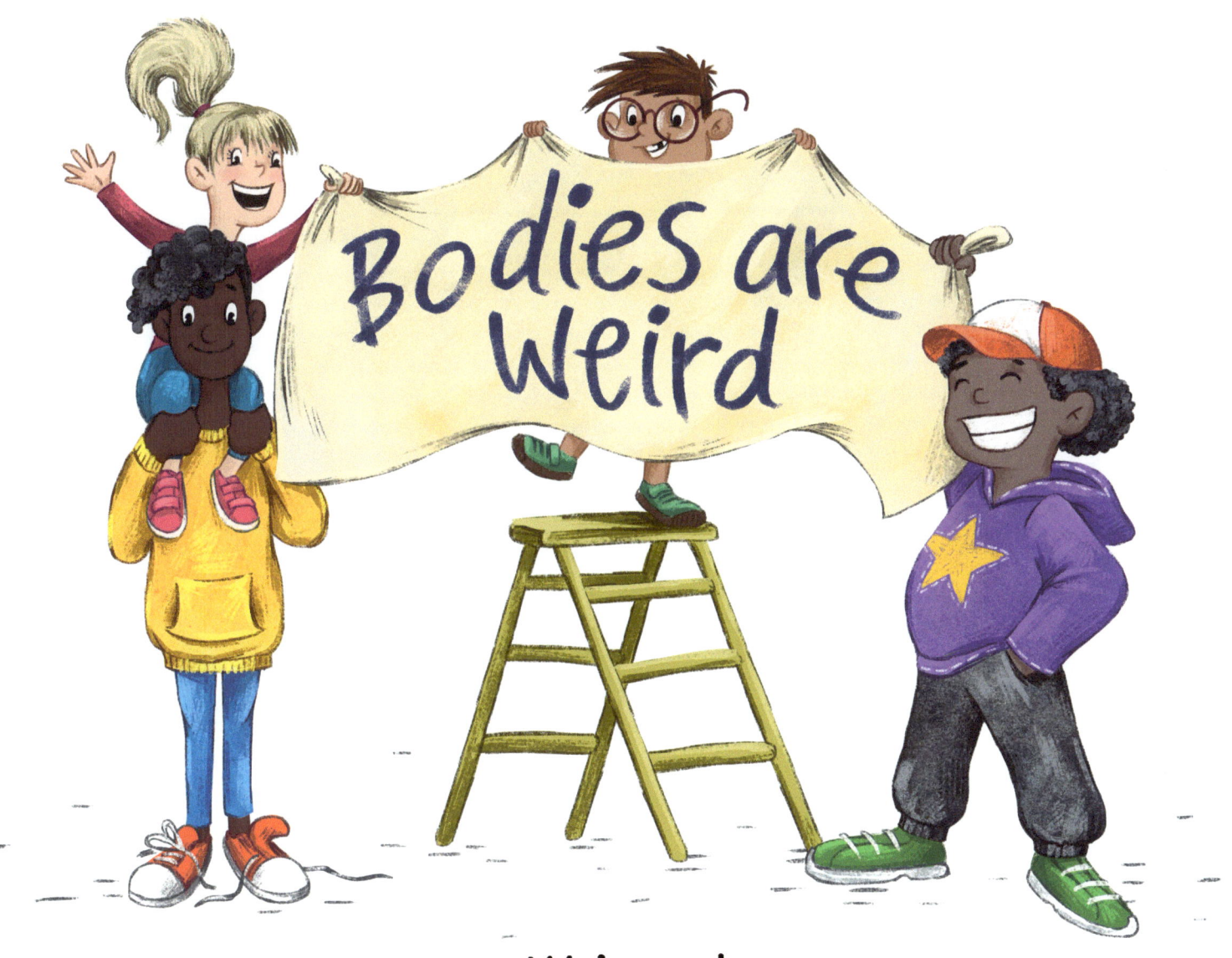

Bodies are Weird

Written by
Megan McGrath & Adam Friedman
Illustrated by Olga Sall

They're short, and they're tall.
They're big, and they're small.

They're different colors, different shapes...

...and some roll, and some crawl.

But there's something you notice
when you look at them all,
whether it's summer or winter...

...or spring or the fall.

Without a doubt, there's one thing that's clear.
No matter what type you have... bodies are weird!

Bodies are weird!
They do funny things,
like goosebumps that rise
when you're so cold it stings.

Hiccups can make you
jump from your seat.
And there are parts that smell funny
like your butt and your feet.

Toes can wiggle, and fingers can too.

And why do
we yawn
when there's
nothing
to do?

When we're shy or ashamed,
our cheeks turn bright red.

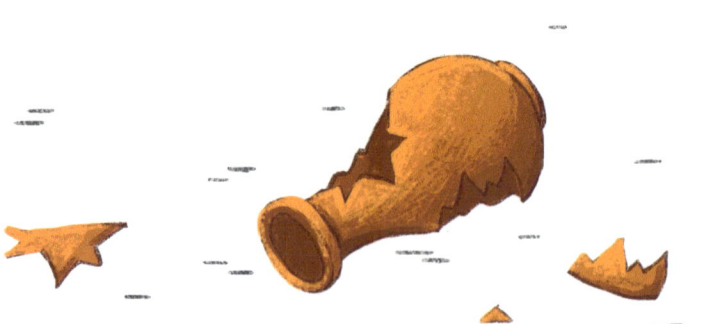

And sometimes our teeth
fall right out of our head.

And how is there wax inside of our ears?
Are there candles inside of us, burning for years?

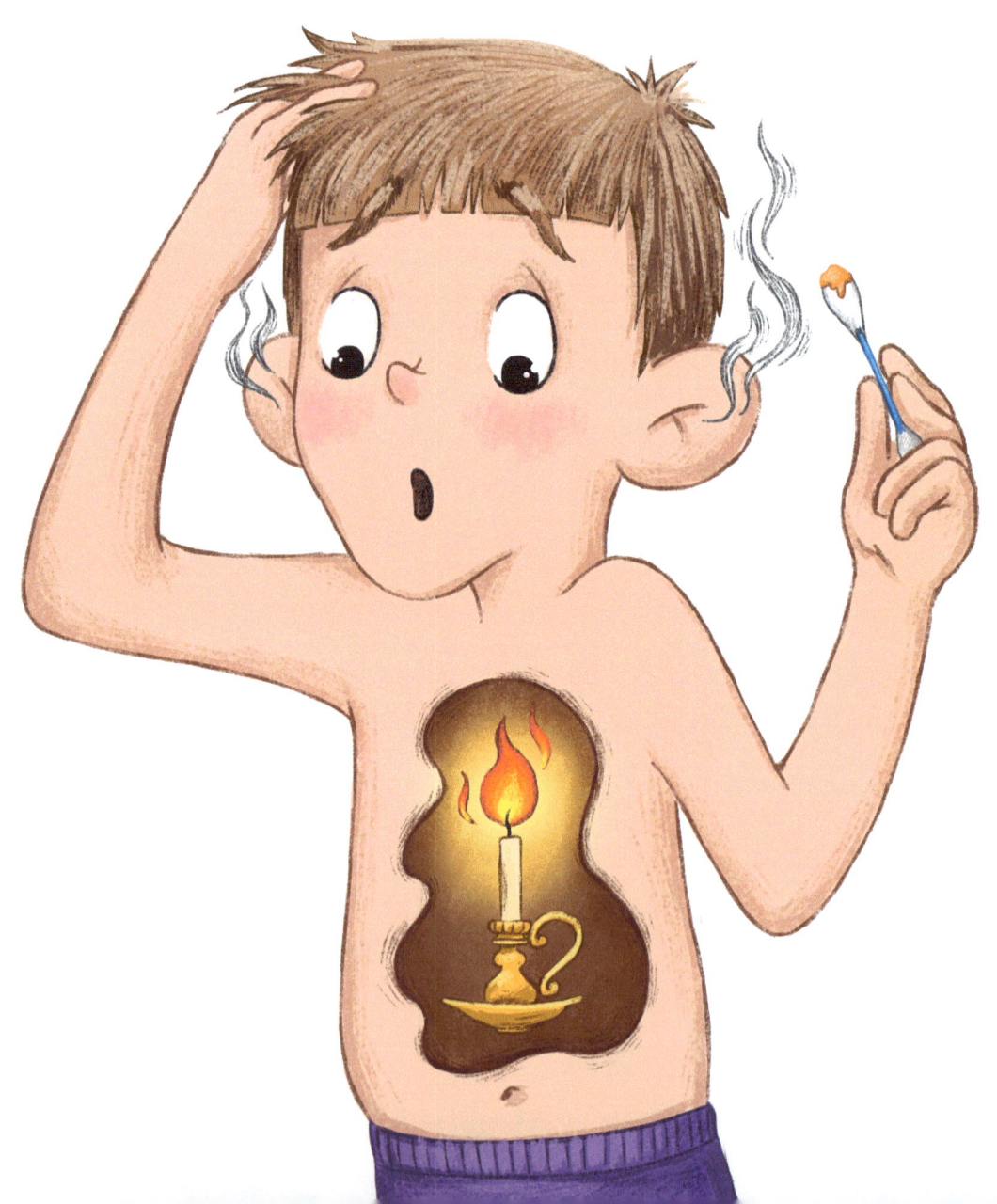

You can cross your eyes,

roll them,

or squint.

And what's with your belly button and all the lint?

When we hear a loud sound,
our heart skips a beat.

And sometimes
we trip over
our own
two feet!

There are freckles and birthmarks
and moles all around.

We could connect all the dots
and see what is found.

There's creaking and cracking
and other sounds too.

When your tummy is growling, it belongs at the zoo!

And I can use my armpit to play **any** song.

The best part is...

... when **you**
play along!

Sometimes we twirl until we fall down.

Our heads feel dizzy, and the world spins around.

Our skin can
burn when
we're out in
the sun.

And isn't it crazy our noses can run?

Funny bones
aren't funny.
No one
knows why.

But tickling
can make
you laugh
till you cry.

And what about farting, tooting, or cutting the cheese?

Feel free to call it whatever you please.

Whatever it's called, it makes quite a sound.
A giggle erupts, and we look all around.

Farting is always a lot of good fun.
But isn't it just a burp from your bum?

Bodies are weird. That's just how it goes.
And we've all got weird stuff that nobody knows.

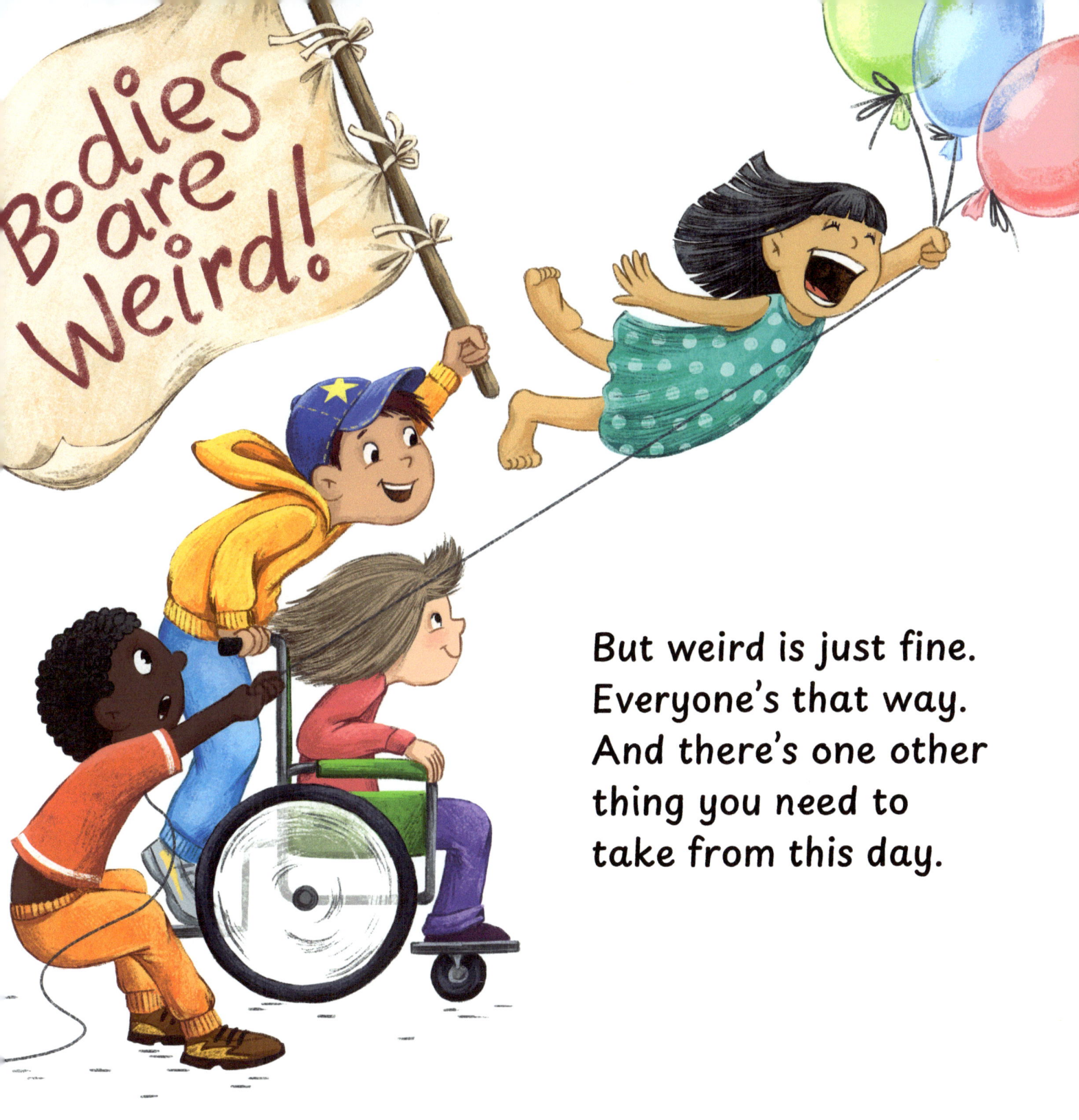

Bodies are weird!

But weird is just fine.
Everyone's that way.
And there's one other
thing you need to
take from this day.

Your body is special.
It's your only one.
So love it,
take care of it,
and have
lots of fun.